al pittman

Thirty-for-Sixty

BREAKWATER
100 Water Street
P.O. Box 2188
St. John's, NF
A1C 6E6

Author and cover photographs by Ray Fennelly.

Canadian Cataloguing in Publication Data

Pittman, Al, 1940–

    Thirty-for-sixty

    (Newfoundland poetry series)

    Poems.
    ISBN 1-55081-154-1

I. Title.   II. Series.

PS8531.I86T45 1999   C811'.542   C99-950226-3
PR199.3.P52T45 1999

The Canada Council | Le Conseil des Arts
for the Arts | du Canada

We acknowledge the financial support of
The Canada Council for the Arts for our publishing activities.

Canada

We acknowledge the financial support of the Government of Canada through the Book Publishing Industry Development Program (BPIDP) for our publishing activities.

Reprinted 2004

Printed in Canada

For Clyde and Simeon Rose

" - in a storm of singing
The voices of all the drowned swam on the wind."

– *Dylan Thomas*

Contents

Another Night in Crawley's Cove

The accordion considers the tunes it knows best.
The conversation, though incoherent, is congenial.

Outside, the balsams are dancing in the wind.
(The branches, an orchestra of castanets.)
Somewhere in the sky, the birds are sound asleep.

The giddy dancers are stepping it out
on the floorboards of their spindrift dreams.

Tomorrow, the music will be still, the sky quiet
and the birds will be back in the backyard woods.

The day will pass without measure until
night falls and time begins again. The birds
will take to the sky, the dreamers to their feet
and the floor will endure or enjoy another night
of jigs, reels, knee-slapping yarns, out-of-tune
tunes and foot-stomping songs.

Elsewhere in the cove there are people asleep.
They'll be up and about before dawn, long before
the last lie has been told and we've all gone
to rest in peace.

The old Waterford wood stove has grown cold.
But there's no discomfort here in this elderly house
on the hill. We are contentedly tired and ready
to creep or crawl to our makeshift beds to await
this day's dawning.

The water, lapping at the landwash, will lull us
to sleep until the birds in the balsams wake us
to another day in Crawley's Cove and another night

close to the floor, well removed from the lives
we live when here is far away. And we are elsewhere.

Where we are the most we have of ourselves.
And the least we have of each other.

♦♦♦

The Citrus Sea

for Tana

Somewhere at sea the oceans shift.
Twenty tons of tropical fruit go overboard.
Tidal waves of lemons floating west.

Wearing only her little laced and latticed
bathing suit, she wobbles to the end of the world.

She's a child. She knows what's real
and what isn't. And now she's about to walk
on water.

Her parents (intent on the intensity
of their efforts to love one another)
are oblivious to the miracle at hand.

Within the seaside, sunlit desperation
of their embrace, they are unaware
that their toddling daughter
is about to alter all they've never known
of themselves and each other.

In the middle of their struggle
for love, she has waded her way
to the edge and end of everything.

The galaxies swirl and curl.
The golden waters beckon.

She trembles in. And goes under.
Comes up splashing in a sea of lemons.
Yellow waves wash over her. She surfaces
for the second time. Goes down for the third.

All this before she knows
what lemons are, what yellow is.

Knowing only what much
there was to know in this world
she has wandered into another
for which she (and they) have no name now.
Nor ever will.

♦♦♦

The Pink, White and Green

for Des Walsh

The flag flat out.
The grass bent south-south-east.
The man mowing the meadow
is no gardener of gardens.
It just happens to be good day
to take care of the country.

The waist-high hay falls away
in sea-green sheets with every swipe
of the stone-honed blade he swings
at the leaning field while cursing
this year's crop of resurrected rocks.

Without a wrinkle in the wind
the flag flies high overhead.

The man mowing the meadow
knows exactly who he used to be
when he took care of his land
without a care for anything
in the world outside those
four fortress fences, fading away now
to the colours of corruption and decay.

He knows the fence needs fixing and
the house uphill, a new coat of paint.
The latch on the garden gate ought to be
replaced, the clothesline pole secured.
But for now, today, there's the land
to be looked after, and the wind
is just right to slice the grass down hill

to the end of the overgrown slope
he's cared for always and only because
it was his and his alone. And theirs.

Back on to the house he's well aware
of his widow up there in the window
watching him sweep the summer's growth of grass
down to the ground, low below
the Pink, White and Green flag
flying high above the only nation
he and she have ever known.

♦♦♦

Lupines

for Frieda

Across the ditch by the graveyard fence
a groundbound rainbow of purple and pink.

Triumphant yesterday in the Trinity Bay sun.
Courageously upright today
in this day's torrential downpour.

I come upon them suddenly
at a quick twist in the twisted road.
Whatever the weather, they are here
this summer season like a bright ribbon
of light, not quite, but almost
out of sight.

Behind and above them, sleeping deep
in the rainsoaked earth, the dead rest
deep in peace.

Below, the waves wash
in their eternal turn upon
the Goose Cove shore.

Making my way to Trinity
in this morning's morning deluge
(soaked to the skin and bereft of love)
I would tip my hat to the trinity
of the sea, the dear departed
and the lupines blooming between.

I don't happen to have a hat on my head
but I do wear a prayer in my heart.

I make a secret Sign of the Cross
and say silently inside to the one god
who doesn't believe in me, "God bless
the long and just gone dead, the sullen
slate-grey sea, and especially (now)
I pray, please bless the lupines blooming there
upright (purple, pink) and right as rain.

♦♦♦

Tuesday's Child

for Ken Livingstone

The best part of any movie
I've ever seen was when "The End"
rolled up or unsuddenly appeared
on the screen as the curtain came down.
And then the slow stroll home.

Late for supper after matinees
or well after dark at night
I'd walk home holding hands
with Tuesday Weld never there.

Then there were those other times
(always) when I was alone without her
nowhere near and very far away. And
I took the long way home past
the four graveyards (on a dark
and lonesome road) terrified of not
being brave enough to do it. And did.

Those were the times I tried to forget
Tuesday Weld and gave up on her
by going alone to The Majestic Theatre
to see "The Curse of Frankenstein".

Christopher Lee played the creature
and shivered the living daylights out of me.
Therefore, I went back and back again.
And therefore, chose the most frightful
way home.

Then, once (having had enough
of death and dead ends), I packed my pack

and hitch-hiked to Hollywood to find
Tuesday Weld, marry her and make her happy.

The closest I came to coming close
was Gary Lockwood, (TV's "Lieutenant")
who I hated on sight because he
was her lover then and I hardly knew
what a lover was or was meant to be.

When I came home to Newfoundland
and The Majestic, I guess I had grown
up some, because, after that, I seldom
went to see the same movie more than
twice in a row.

I might have gone glad to be frightened
by "The Bride of Frankenstein"
three or four times. But none of those times
did I take the graveyard road home.

Neither have I (ever since) held hands
with Tuesday Weld or gone to Hollywood
in search of any love or everlasting lust.

I may have kept the compulsion
of my vagrant and virtuous ways.
But that journey (then) had no beginning.

Here's where it ended. And here
is where it won't begin again.

Unless never begins again, and
I yet have love enough to spend
weeks in the weather on the side
of a highway going nowhere with

nowhere to go but here, holding
hands with the lone and lonesome
dead. All the way home to home.

♦♦♦

The Joy of Cooking

for Michael Ondaatje

"I am the cinnamon peeler's wife.
Smell me."

It isn't exactly that I wish
I had written the poem
that winds its way
with such fragrant passion
to those last lines. It has
more to do with my aspirations
in the kitchen.

No matter what I'm cooking
I am always out of cinnamon.

I live on an island in the North Atlantic.
The back yard affords no advantage.

What I serve my guests (my unlikely lovers)
is a lot less than what I'd gladly offer them.

For this uncertain occasion
I've prepared an adequate meal.
John the Baptist's head has been marinating
in the fridge for three days.
Now it's on the table and Salome Smith
and I are ready to dine.

It promises not to be another wasted weekend.

Tentatively she takes the tiniest taste.
Then the lovely Ms. Smith looks at me
(seduction written all over) and says
"This is delicious".

It isn't bad. But it would have been better
had I had any cinnamon in the house.
We finish with a toast to love.
I say "Grace After Meals".

We leave John's half-eaten head
on the table with the dishes
and the homemade pickles.
And go to bed,

"Would you read me a recipe?" she pleads.
I reach under the pillow and pull out
Ondaatje's book of poems.

By the time I get to the end
of "The Cinnamon Peeler"
she is sound asleep.

The Baptist's skull and dirty dishes
are still out there on the kitchen table.

That was Friday.
It's been a long, lonely weekend in bed.

Tomorrow being Monday
I must remember to pick up
some cinnamon, and a copy
of the poet's other gourmet guide:
"There's a Trick With a Knife I'm Learning To Do".

That could come in handy in the kitchen.
Or in bed. Either way it wouldn't do any harm
to have it at hand. That, some cinnamon
and a good sharp knife.

♦♦♦

Hard Times

In the middle of a dream
he rolled out of bed
and died that night
stabbed to death
by a bottle he'd broken
in his fatal fall
to the flop-house floor.

There in a dump
called "The American Hotel"
in New York City
he left his blood
for some weary maid
to clean up after him.

There in the crimson smear
at the end of a dream, far, far
from The Swanee River. Far
from the magnolia blooming south
of his songs, Stephen Foster
came to no good end.

There, between destitution and death
his hard times dissolved in darkness.
Then and thereafter they could come
again no more.

Too long had they lingered
around that dead-end door.

"Hard times, hard times come again no more".

♦♦♦

Standing Room Only

I tell this not as I would in Confession
but without a word of a lie.

At the height of his golden trumpeting
"High Society" career of fame
and fortune, Louis Armstrong waved
his famous cotton kerchief at me
from a bandstand in a hockey rink
in Corner Brook, Newfoundland.

That was the night I declined to go
to Hell for the sake of love then or thereafter.

Danny Barcelona played the drums.
Satchmo played his golden horn
and sang deep down to all the lovers
he'd ever and never known, while
Susan and I danced to the magic
of the music and all things so suddenly possible.

At intermission we went for a ride
in my father's old Oldsmobile. The music
had made the promise of everything
come true. In the old quarry where we
parked, we held on to each other like lovers
on the brink of love until it came
to toss-up time between time and Eternity.

That's when I stammered (stupidly)
"We'd better get back".

Without a word all the way, we returned
to the rink, rigged out for the night like
a nightclub in Monte Carlo or Hollywood.

That's the last I saw of Susan. She (and
whoever he was) danced one dance
after another while I sat forlorn, alone
on a bench in the bleak bleachers
above and beyond the end of the dream
that was never to be anything but.

When I turned away from what I had forsaken
down there on the flood-lit floor, I saw a sign
that read "Standing Room Only".

Danny Barcelona beat out a solo
that would have made Gene Krupa
roll over. Louis Armstrong wiped
his brow with his sweat-wet trademark
and waved it at me where I sat, sad and
solitary, in the empty attic of the night.

I waved my applause back at him.
He lifted his horn and blew one
long lilting note that faded finally
in the dim rafters low overhead.

And that's the note I left on.

Driving my father's Rocket '88
home, I held on to the steering wheel
for dear life and to my immortal soul
for all and what little it was worth.

Louis Armstrong has since died.
Susan has since married. I am
still alive without a hope
in hell of ever going to Heaven.

Remembering that night, I recall lying
wide awake in bed (the car parked
secure, inviolate in the driveway)
and remember God the Father
whispering at me through the metal mesh window
dividing the double dark closets
in which we were confined as though
we were locked together in Limbo.

I confessed my temptation without a fib.
Father So-and-so said "Ego te absolvo".
And then, "For your penance say three Hail Marys".

The absolution granted, the penance
prescribed, there in the dark of that dismal
dungeon, I was blessed and dismissed
to an eternity of celibate sainthood.

I've prayed a lot of prayers since then.
And spent a lot of time kneeling on my knees.

But also since, I've promised myself, Satchmo
(and all the saints who've gone marching in)
that long before the last blast of the trumpet
sounds, I'll be among the lowest of the low-down
dancers below here and hereafter.

And that's a promise I promise to keep
until my knees give out or the music stops.

Having spent so much time in a state
of grace, Heaven hardly seems worth the effort.

Therefore I have resolved to "Go and sin
no more." And almost haven't.

♦♦♦

Touching You

Touching you is to touch
what remains of passion past.
The loveliest love we are to know
is that that will never last.

Past lovers lie in beds of clay
deep beneath our feet.
Their love, for them, though new and true
was measurably complete.

What destinies you and I embrace
are certain. That's for sure.
In virtue we are very rich.
In rapture rather poor.

♦♦♦

The Moon Also Rises

Now in mid-January, the new year
young, the moon as old and cold
as ancient iron rusting in the sky
may be but some blot or blur
on the window pane above where
I lie tilted to Heaven praying
my pagan prayers to the gods of Love.

Or the stars are but some celestial illusion
blinking in blank succession out of sight.

Without a breeze this edge of anywhere
(to torment them to their dark distress)
the barren lilacs rattle in the restless wind.

I strive for dreams to dream
but the slow corrosion of the moon, the quick
going of the stars and the confusion
of the demented trees exhaust me
beyond any sleep's relief.

Now dawn breaks and the sun
ascends above a blank blanket of cloud.

The sky (charcoal grey, dull as death)
threatens good weather. Expecting no response
from the gods and goddesses to whom I pray
and knowing nothing good can come
on a morning in the middle of a night such
as this, I twist and turn to hold my wrinkled
pillow tight. And pray, with all my might, it
were smoothly you, sleeping alongside, quietly

breathing. Yet I wish you a deep sleep
and sunshine when and wherever you wake
in darkness or in daylight and in whose arms
you've chosen for the embrace you need
now and would wish to encircle you
the rest of your loving life.

♦♦♦

This Side of Heaven
for Raylene and the rest of the Rankins

Here's where it happens.
And where else is love "likely to go better"?
Where else could we expect
to find such mortal measurements
as death provokes us to defy?

Where else a lilac tree's brief bloom?
(The purple orchard's quick decay.)
The burst of a berry's colour on the tongue?

Nowhere beyond here are there medicines
to mend the broken heart or dull the dullest
pain. Nowhere else is known the flight
of birds, the eclipse of ecstacy. The coming
together and the ripping goodbyes beneath
the blankets - the layers of despair we wear
to keep love warm.

All the colours of love and loss thrive here
under this dome of sky where we breathe
farewell with every breath.

"Fare thee well, Love."

As long as you live this side of Heaven
forever fare thee well.
Only here has Heaven any need of angels
or any need of us to be their guardians.

And here's only where we
might do our best to be so. And be.

♦♦♦

The Sea Breeze Lounge

It's a warm overcast Bonne Bay afternoon.
There's a slight north-east breeze on the water.
Inside, Black Hat George is tending bar.
He, myself, and one other patron are the only
people here. The younger man has made his way
to the gambling machine with the aid of some
awkward machinery designed to keep him
upright. A truck ran over him in Toronto
and he's come home to learn to walk again.

The pool table stands staunch on its crutches.
The juke box is silent, all its hurtin' songs
sung to silence because pain can be fatal
and machines and people do break down.

Of course, I'm here too, about to give up
and perhaps give out for good. But for now
I'm one of three survivors who've almost
survived so far. Almost isn't a good feeling
but it shall have to do for now. You are
(my dearest darling, wherever you are)
surviving like the rest of us. I would like
to be of some assistance but the hazards
that have brought me here drag me down
like a heavy harness, an iron cross.

There's not much comfort but plenty
of solitude in The Sea Breeze this overcast
afternoon. There's a determined young man
learning to walk again. There's George
who wears his black hat with wild-west

authority. He has one leg left and a vigorous
hop in every step he takes down the seaside
street at high noon, sunset or any time of day.
And there's me, the picture of health
and wholeness (scared to death to stand up
lest I fall flat on my face).

I think it's worth it, whatever else our obstinate
ailments are, that we don't fall down, that all three
of us (and you) do our best to walk upright
and go with hope to wherever we are bound.

Right now I know we three could use a drink.
And this round's on me. But, most of all as far
from here as you happen to be this round's
a toast to you, your agility and your vigorous ascent
to the top of your dreams.

♦♦♦

Gnomes

Every time I spring awake and look
out this window I see gnomes hanging
in the trees. They have red or purple
hair and green beards. And terribly
twisted faces. They have no bodies.
They are grotesque, gargoyled heads
hanging and swinging in the mild, wild
south-west summer wind.

As much as I like things floral and full
of leaves, I'd not go near those blossoms
without a weapon to combat their threats
now or any other night like this.

Whoever strolls, staggers or stumbles by
will be devoured before they know they
are gone or what it was that ended them.

These are flowers, adorable in daylight.
They are the gifts you'd give to your
mothers, your lovers, or to your friends
in need of anything delightful to happen.

But on nights such as this they eat people.
They live outside (and close by) my
bedroom window. Therefore I sleep
wide awake with all the doors and windows
locked. And not a breath of air to breathe.

All these summer nights I suffocate safely.
Knowing when morning comes, the gnomes
will be flowers again and bouquets to give.

◆◆◆

Wanderlust

I like the word "wanderlust".
"Love" is nice too but I like lust most
because love compels you
to stay places you want to be.

Lust, on the other hand, takes you
places you'd never venture to go
without longing not to be where
you are. And (when you get there)
it's not all that hard to find
your way back.

Coming away from love is a difficult
descent from the summit of yourself
back to base camp and the basics
that await you there. Though love can
be "a many splendored thing", it's about
halfway back you find yourself wishing you
had never gone that high in the beginning.

Lust is kinder to the wanderer
(the armchair nomad who spends
all his lifetimes reading the maps
of those he'd love forever
if only he could ascend to them).

But apart from such silly and sensible
considerations as these. "Wanderlove"
just doesn't do what a word
should do. Whereas, "Wanderlust" does.

It speaks the language of love
on foreign, far-off tongues and
requires no translation.

♦♦♦

Lambs to the Slaughter

She told me this twice.

There were lambs prancing
in the pasture. And it was
coming on slaughter time.

She was fond of the cows
(goats, roosters and corn).
But she dearly adored the lambs.

She knew what little and as much
as she could (in her little age) about
life and death on her father's farm.
And even then she knew the lambs
would never grow up to be sheep.
But above all, she wanted to be
there the day they went. It would have been
a time never to be forgotten.

She hadn't seen anything killed except
carrots and cabbages and trees. The only
blood she'd ever seen had been her own
and that of some Sunday supper's hen.

Counting the days (without knowing
what day) she went to sleep each night
reciting the litany of the names
she had named the lambs.

When the day came, she was sent away
to an uncle's acres many miles down
the road to spend the afternoon playing
make-believe with her cousins.

Her father (aware of her love for the lambs)
had decided the death of them ought to be
done in her absence. And when her uncle
ushered her in the door (the afternoon gone)
it was all over. Death was done.

She hasn't since forgiven her father
for having taken that day out of her life.

"I don't hate him", she said.
"I just can't forgive him".

She told me this twice. Once before
and once after. And there, in the sadness
of her sad grip, I wept for her, for her father
and all things (like that night) gone for good
and too close to get back to ever again.

♦♦♦

Rites of Passage

for Janice and Gerard

Whatever little time we live, time
in the end, adds up to no time at all.
Sadly and gladly there are things
to be seen in the sun and missed
in flight along the way.

We take to wing, fly a while, ponder
all that circles below us and descend
to earth. We look up to see where
we've been. We measure the spaces
we inhabit inside, out and about.

The ground beneath our feet
is our foothold for as long as we
can stand and hang on. The sky
is where birds and angels dwell.
We've all been visitors there and come
back home to the back yards of Heaven.

The sky is where we've been when
we've gone to sleep undreaming
or been wide awake, night and day
alert to our own mortality.

But however low below the slow clouds
we strive to thrive, the sun burns above.

And keeps on burning.

♦♦♦

Brimstone Head

From here, looking north, there's nothing
to see but the sea. And in winter, nothing
but blue-white ice glowing and flowing
from here to the polar ocean. It's a sight
to behold and a long way from here to
nowhere north of here.

A lot of lives have been lost out there.

The North Atlantic (as majestic as it is)
has a grim history. But now, in the safety
of the sun, we lie here on this headland
in a patch of partridge berry leaves
and behold the wonder we behold
as we hold each other with no end
in sight and all the world stretching north
to nowhere we shall ever go, ever stay, or
ever have to come home from.

◆◆◆

Sunshower after Dark

You stride by at a glance, a rainbow
in your hair. There's a shower of sun
falling from heights heavens above
the ground-bound worlds we live in.
Together, the sun and the rain
adorn you from head to earth.

You go by in a slight sight
of time, but time and sight
enough to imagine you as I do
when I close my eyes and see you
clothed in moonlight, dressed only
in darkness, star-stepping across the sky.

You stride by. I blink. You are gone.
And I am left with a glance to remember
long after the sun goes down and long
after it rises to brighten up another day.

Of course, it never rains but it pours.
Tonight there's a leak in the roof
above my bed. The room is full of
"cats and dogs" and "buckets" and full
of you walking in the rain with the sun
from the ceiling lighting up your hair.

Curled beneath my wet tent
of blankets, I can't see you.
But still I perceive (as in a mist)
you striding by out of sight, out
of reach, up the road, gleaming
in the dark, rainshine glistening
in your hair.

The sun is now on the rise in a sky
with no horizon. And where you
are, there is no rain. And nothing to fall
that hasn't been heaven-sent, bright
and brighter than sunshine after dark.

◆◆◆

Erin's Pub
for Ralph O'Brien

Ralph is tending bar and doing the bar's
business bookwork. He greets me with a smile.
It's the first time I've seen him since his wife
so recently died. He's in a good mood
and I am glad for him. He hasn't been broken
by the ordeals of illness and death he's endured.

We exchange our familiar greetings, he accepts
my condolence and we go about our own stuff.
He, coping with accounts and such matters
as business demands. Me, scribbling a poem
bound for the waste-paper basket.

Ralph is a son of Erin who's emigrated here
to Newfoundland by virtue of his voice.
He's a singer of high degree and sings
his ancestral soul within and out with every song.

He's been around and somehow come to settle
here where he's found something to sustain
his rambling spirit and his love for all things home.

Eventually we get together and talk
of his wife's death, his daughter's
loss, his own bereavement. Congenially
he does his best to assure me (or himself)
that all is well and everyone's fine. For
the sake of good manners, I take him
at his word. We drink a toast to each other
and to those who have gone from the pub
(the street) and the face of the earth.

Ralph returns to his bookwork. I go back
to my waste-paper poem. One of his songs
is playing in the background. It's enough.
There are no words needed and none to be
said until we shake hands, say "See you soon".

And I go out the door to a street
congested with young and would-be lovers
going nowhere together. And daylight all abroad.

♦♦♦

Intruder

Walking by the house
on the corner, I turn into
the path, go up the steps
and open the door like
I would have then.

I haven't forgotten that you
live elsewhere. But I do
remember the years inside.
And, too late, I realize that
those who live here now
don't know me from Adam
or the neighbours next door.

They don't know I just stopped in
to say "Hello" to someone they've
never known and can't imagine.

But, suddenly, there's this stranger
standing before them muttering
apologies they can't comprehend.

The children (about their childhood)
presume I'm a plumber or someone
efficient and effective at pipes and things.
Their parents suffer my rude intrusion
and do their best to turn their backs
back to the immediacy of their lives.

As best their bewilderment
and my embarrassment will
allow, I make my awkward exit

like a child who hasn't yet
learned to walk or talk as I go
stumbling, stuttering into the dark.

This invasion isn't a habit.
Yet it might make someone wonder.

And I wonder what those parents
tell their children about people
who think with their feet and have
no notion of where they're going.
Or where they live. Or why.

I hope (all the way from there
to nowhere) that none of this
makes any difference to this couple
or their children.

They haven't lived there all that long
and may move again anytime soon.

Then, with their furniture, their memories
and their lives rearranged to suit
their new surroundings, just before
supper, one of the children says
"Remember the man with the whiskers
who used to come to our home
looking for something? I wonder
if he ever found whatever it was
he was looking for".

And another younger youngster says
"At least he didn't steal the gerbils
or eat the budgie bird!"

"Of course not," says Mr. So-and-So.
"He might have been crazy, but he
wasn't all that crazy. Don't we
all, sometimes, go looking
for something we've lost?"

He's about to pass the gravy, when
his wife (having said nothing so far)
says, smiling "Yes! Don't we, Darling?"

Then they say "Grace" and carry on.

♦♦♦

Home on The Heights

for Marilee

This house becomes you.
You wear it
like flannel, satin or silk.

It wraps around you.

And you move inside
as some lover might move
in the arms of a lover -
the passion as apparent
as the swing of swings
and things in motion.

The palatial halls of Vienna
would envy this house
these humble walls.

How they bend with grace
to greet you. The way you sway
within. How the whole house
moves with you.

And you with it.
As you swing and sway
waltzing your way
from wall to wall
all the way home.

♦♦♦

Christening

Choosing a name for our unborn child
we peruse all the Name Your Baby books
we can find. One from the local library.
One from a supermarket checkout rack.
One borrowed from a friend who's had
two miscarriages. (The futile considerations
underlined in crayon.)

The books begin with names like Aaron
and end with names like Zephaniah.
Thousands of possibilities!
We consider the names of relatives too.
Parents, grand-parents, great-grand-parents.
Uncles, aunts, cousins, nephews
and nieces. And without the dubious benefit
of ultra-sound to define the gender of our dreams
we consider male and female names.
But nothing from any of these sources seems
inevitably right to be what this child
shall be called for the rest of life's promise.

So we go ambling through our own histories.
And there we come upon the place where
I received my father's name because I was
the first born of his several sons and he
was obliged to observe the traditions
of his place and time. Thus I became
Alphonsus James Peter Pittman.

The place was St. Kyran's, so called
after one of three eccentric Irish saints.

Abandoned by government decree
St. Kyran's is now a seaside remnant of ruins.
But for the splintered church's spectral spire
still pointing sky-high to the heavens
above Placentia Bay, you might never know
anyone had ever been born or ever died there.

Centuries ago in far off Ireland
a man maddened by Christianity
hobbled throughout the land with a cow
as his only companion. His purpose to convert
the infidel Celts. So St. Kyran's got its name.

And so did our daughter get hers.
Before she was born, she inherited
a name with a history. Not of Ireland
or its lunatic saints but with the history
of the time and place wherein she was bred
to be born. Destined to be. Kyran.
Child of history. Child of mystery.
Child of mine.

♦♦♦

A Bouquet for Emily

These frail flowers will not last
the length of your journey.
They'll not stay in bloom long enough
to decorate your destination
or bless your destiny with blossoms.

They are buttercups given only
to lament the gladness of your going.

As you always have, you will go
on tip-toe, summer-saulting
and cart-wheeling all the way.

These fragile flowers will wilt
long before this beginning begins.

But whatever awaits you (wherever
you go) won't matter as long
as what fate rains down on you
is as golden as these petals are now
and as you have been in all seasons
beneath the meadows in the sky
lighting the fields with love and laughter
upsidedown and homeward bound
ever brighter than the brightest light.

I shall be forever fond of those fields
and the flowers blooming there wild
(with you within) as I walk among them
bending the long grass in the shadow
of your green and golden glow.

Because there's little else to offer
(now as you depart) I pass you
this fistful of flowers, wish you
heaps and leaps of love, lots of luck
and quiet smiles all the way home.
Always with buttercups growing
from the ground up and the sky down.

♦♦♦

My Daughters Write Poems

You do the best you can.
But there are no guarantees.

Most of my friends have children
who have children. Some of their children
have children and geraniums
and dogs and lawn mowers.

Not so my daughters.
They live in phone booths
and telephone me poems
in the middle of the night.

I want to say "I'm sorry.
I should have been a better father".
I want to plead "Please
let me be so before I die".

"I'll wallpaper your living room.
I'll build you a bird house.
I'll drown the kittens.
I'll tell all the right lies".

I want to say "Please, forgive me".

But their words
enforce a certain silence.

I go back to bed
lullabyed to sleep
with my daughters in my arms
and their poems in my mouth.

♦♦♦

To Kyran in Full Flight

The borders you must cross to get to Mexico
are nothing compared to the borders
you've crossed to get to where you are.

Going toward yourself is
the longest journey of all.

There are instruments to help you
get to San Miguel de Allende.
But the southbound bird winging
its way south without map or compass
holds within its heart some knowing
unknown even to itself.

Your lover awaits your arrival
in full knowledge that you have been
his destiny all along. The artist
who painted your portrait portrayed you
as a bird imprisoned on its perch.
Your expression there -
the grim anticipation of flight.

Now (fold upon fold of that feathered grip let go)
you've taken to wing. Now you have no instruments
to guide you. And now your destination
has nothing to do with Mexico.

The horizons tumble away as they leap-frog
forever forward in front of you. Your journey
is the journey that has no end.

I will miss you. And I will envy your lover
his destiny under the ancient Aztec sun.
But as long as you travel the endless skyways

to (and ever toward) your heart's delight
I'll be there with you, soaring somewhere
alongside – winging it all the way.

♦♦♦

The Annunciation

You, my lovely daughter (your
immaculately conceived conception
concealed by all but the bulge
of your belly, curtained
by your blessed flesh, hidden
from the world about to be born
into the world-wide warmth
of your embrace are here now
on the eve of everything
this while before the world turns
and their is no returning.

Somewhere along the way
we've all been born. And always
there've been mothers and fathers
and the umbilical beginning
of all things future, holy and profane.

Your child is yours now only
for this tiniest of times. Soon
the tidal-wave world will spill in
and this wonder will ebb
as your wishes wash, spread
and splash over cradle and crib
and the world's turning tide
outruns your child's first footsteps
up the kelp-covered landwash
to the wind-bent meadow
where little mice hunt, hide and seek
and there is life and sudden death
then, there and ever thereafter.

There'll be photographs of your father.
Stories to tell. Yarns to spin.
And songs to sing. All barely credible
and none of them true. Except you.

You shall be the truth of me alive
as once I was when my father lived
never to live happily ever after in love
with grass, trees, snow, all things in bloom
and children outdoors in all seasons.

Then, the yard and the woods around
overflowed with birds and animals.
Swarms of insects, rain, hail, snow
and sunshine and bats by the billions
filled the air and the swift swallows
swooped over the river that flowed
ever west where the heavens bent
gently to genuflect below the slow, low
hanging clouds on the high horizon.

There, on the edge of eternity
by the eternal river, we'd lie silent
on the slant, sand-banked beach
and peer deep down into the dark
and bottomless starlit sky.

Now, there's this new and other
high horizon for you, your child and us
(all your long-lost and everlasting lovers).

But look! In the dark and starless sky
this north November night, the sun
is rising here where your sanctity shines

within and shall shine for as long as
infinity lasts and forever is.

For "Blessed is the fruit of thy womb".
And thee.

♦♦♦

Homecoming
for Alden

You are too lately born
to know where you are.

Arkansas! Newfoundland!
What's the difference but for
the immediacy of the floor
beneath your face, the familiar
comfort of the foreign bed
you share, always aware
of what's within your ever groping grasp?

One day you'll know all you'll want
to know about Newfoundland. And
maybe, some other day, you'll return.
Your Arkansas friends may ask
"Where y'all going?"

"Newfoundland", you'll reply
 as though it were somewhere
just up there in The Ozarks.

"Where's that?"

"It's an island in the sky
just north of the Northern Star
and it's full of fairies, ghosts
and goblins. It's as old as the stars
(as cold as ice) and warm as embers.

"When will you be back?"

"Sometime! Soon! But I gotta go now
and ask my mom if she'll wrap and roll

my carpet. I'm off to Newfoundland
first thing in the morning."

"See ya!"

"See y'all, soon."

Then you'll take off and land nowhere
on Earth and feel whatever you feel
at home on a starlit beach dancing
with the the fairies, the ghosts and goblins
by the slap-happy sea as the Blomidon Mountains
dive deep down to the water's waltzing edge
and The Northern Lights sing in the sky
to welcome you, as we do now and will
whenever you return here to here.

To the fairies, the ghosts, the goblins. And to us.

♦♦♦

A River Runs Through Her

Coming on dark, the loons lament
the slow closing of the sky. And she's
out there having one more flick.

The rod, the reel, the line
are extensions of her self.

Here (hidden in twilight)
I watch from the river bank
and wonder what some stranger
might think if she were his mother
out there in that current
going for the legal limit
at age eighty-three.

Would he stand here in the shelter
of these trees where I stand safe
on shore shielding myself from the realities
that surround me, and think "That's my mother.
She's the flow my father swam in"?

The last cast. The feathered fly afloat.
The sudden splash. The leap of the heart.
The frantic landing.

She rows ashore in the dawn of dark.

I leave the trees, the loons and the river
and slip away in the sudden comfort
of darkness.

I am the stranger.

Though she is my mother
I know nothing of this woman.
I know only that a river runs through her.

And I splash in her blood like a fish.

♦♦♦

The Fuller Brush Man

Behind the bar
your day's work done
you've just released your hair
from its rhinestone shackle.

Now it shines in these shadows
like moonlight on water
(starshine in the darkest night)
and when you move it shimmers
from your waist up like a veil
of sequins, diamonds or gold dust.

From here where I sit remembering
I see some several strands gone astray.

And now (only) I permit myself
to imagine my fingers imagining
themselves deliberately and delicately
brushing each wayward wisp
of your hair back into place
(as they take all the time in the world
never getting to the end of anything).

I am remembering once upon a time
when my father was the Fuller Brush man.
His hands brushed my mother's hair
to beauty beyond his own belief
(until his hands died in her hair).
Broke and broken hearted
he left my mother nothing
but the legacy of his marvelous love.

Had you been born when I knew him
he would have welcomed your hair
into his hands as I would (now)
reach out of reach for all things lovely.

And now I learn you haven't been working
behind the bar all day. You've just come
from your father's funeral.

Your encounter with death today
was fuller than that my skeletal hands
would have woven in your hair
for the sake of selling myself
another brush with death –
the guaranteed going of all things
as beautiful as my mother's hair
as passionate as my father's hands –
moonlight on water
(starshine in the darkest night).

♦♦♦

Thirty-for-Sixty

My father was a man of metaphors.
When he said to me, "Don't wait
until you have the five in your hand
before you go thirty-for-sixty"
he wasn't talking about cards.

Newfoundland's national pastime
is a game of Growl (otherwise called
Auction or A Hundred and Twenties).
Thirty-for-sixty is the ultimate bid.
To make that bid without the five
of trumps in your hand is a foolish
thing to do. Chances are (nine times
out of ten) you'll end up in the hole.

So what! When it's just a game.
A bit of fun. What the hell!

But that night as he lay dying
he wasn't talking about cards.
No overdose of morphine
could diminish his need to leave
his son one last word of wisdom.

I listened and took him to heart.

I've been going thirty-for-sixty
without the five ever since.

The hole grows deeper and deeper.

And now it's my turn to bid again.

I don't have the five in my hand
and I've little else to go on.

But what the hell!

Thirty-for sixty!

♦♦♦

www.ingramcontent.com/pod-product-compliance
Lightning Source LLC
LaVergne TN
LVHW021547080426
835509LV00019B/2880